FINDING MEANING IN A TEETER-TOTTER WORLD

Mark D. Sauter

"Your purpose in life is to find your purpose and give your whole heart and soul to it."

- Gautama Buddha

Studies repeatedly report increases in depression, suicide, hypertension, obesity, addiction, violence, and workplace discontent.

Billions of dollars are being spent attempting to reverse these trends only to discover that they are getting worse.

This book will define what is missing. As the image of a teeter-totter conveys, a meaningful and healthy life requires balance: weight on both sides in order to make the ride enjoyable. One side reflects our more visible, outer values in terms of wealth, status, influence and pleasure. The other side reflects our inner values in terms of self-growth, relationships, and sense of purpose or contribution to others.

Today, many people are out of balance. Thanks to our mega-mall, multi-media society, many people believe happiness and a greater sense of meaning can be achieved by continually adding more and more weight to one-side – the external or material side. In this way, they are defined by where they live, what they do, own, drive or wear. This may initially be enough for some people. For others, they realize something is missing, yet they can't put their finger on what.

This book will shed light on the 'other' side of a meaningful and happy life, which is one's intrinsic need for hope, purpose and love.

Neither side is superior. Instead, it is about balance. This book will initially show how this 'other' side will positively influence our overall health, energy and vitality. This will be followed by what organizations can do to foster balance and thereby improve workplace effectiveness, health and vitality.

Confucius believed that sustainable social improvement *is conditioned by an individual's group relationships* and therefore *must occur where people spend the majority of their time*. Many people today spend the majority of their time at work.

© Copyright 2013 Mark D. Sauter

Bringing Meaning into Monday™ is a trademark of
GTP Associates, Inc.

All Rights Reserved

Printed in the United States of America by:

CreateSpace
100 Enterprise Way, Suite A200
Scotts Valley, CA 95066

ISBN 978-1-449-544546

Table of Contents

The Other Side 8
Soaring … 10
Improving Health & Vitality 12
    Emotional Health 14
    Social Health 16
    Spiritual Health 18
Live, Work, Play 20
Why Work, Why Now 22
Bringing Meaning into Monday™ 26
Impact on Me 28
The Role of Leadership 30
    Achieving More with Less 32
    The Essence of Work – Creating Value 34
    Getting on the Same Page – Unity 36
Going Forward 38
A Picture Says a 1000 Words 40
A Closing Word 42
Note from the Author 44

The Other Side

The 'other,' more intrinsic side of life's teeter-totter is not about having a particular belief, religion or deciding where or if you worship a higher power. Instead, it is about using your life, your circumstances, and your relationships with others, good and bad, to discover and shape your inner-sense of purpose. Psychologists refer to this process as self-actualization, and most spiritual traditions speak of an essence at the center of us. It is what most call God and others call a Higher Power, the Soul, the Divine, the Sacred, the Spirit, or the Essence, and it represents who we are at the core. Commitment to something larger than our own success provides our lives with a greater sense of meaning and purpose. This is what Christians call "stewardship" and Buddhists call "right livelihood."

Many people have lost touch with the essence of life. We all have an intrinsic need to seek purpose, meaning, hope, and a connection to something bigger than ourselves. This inner-quest defines the other side – discovering what makes you tick. Everyone has an inner-dream or purpose. It exists, yet it is largely undeveloped because many people are out of balance – consumed by the pleasures and pain of everyday life.

Achieving balance requires cultivation of both internal and external traits and characteristics. Adding weight or emphasis to the internal is not about denying the importance of the material fruits of life. Instead, it is about being more intentional in adding weight to our internal being by improving the quality of our relationships and commitment to inner-growth. In so doing, we mindfully make positive contributions to the lives of others and/or the greater good. In this way, people will see obstacles and opposition as opportunities for self-growth and a chance to discover and shape their intrinsic sense of purpose or destiny.

The challenge, unfortunately, remains. Thanks to our societal emphasis on the "more-is-better" mentality, and the well-intentioned pull of family and friends, it is easy to lose sight of this other, more private side.

> *Like so many Americans, she was trying to construct a life that made sense from things she found in gift shops.*
>
> - Kurt Vonnegut, Novelist
> *Slaughterhouse Five*

Soaring ...

If life were like a hot-air balloon, our success – our ability to soar – would be dependent on something we don't necessarily see: wind. We have a choice. We can work with the wind or attempt to go against it.

The reality is each of us does have a hot-air balloon residing inside of us; that is colorful and unique. It reflects our sense of purpose or dreams.

Unfortunately, for many of us, our inner-balloon remains crated up and stored in a dark part of a rather cluttered garage called life. While accessible, our balloon remains unseen, undeveloped, and therefore unfulfilled.

> *"It is not enough to be busy; so are the ants. The question is: what are we busy about?"*
>
> – Henry David Thoreau

In addition to everyday living, our life's goal should be about uncrating our inner-balloon, allowing it to soar. This inner-quest is what will give our life purpose, energy, focus, and a greater sense of meaning. Rewarding? Yes, but not easy.

Discovering our inner-balloon is the first step; however, in order for it to soar, the tethers that are holding it back must be removed. Reconciling tethers, such as self doubts, unresolved hurts or rejections, toxic relationships, and most difficult of all, pride, will ultimately determine the degree in which we soar.

Many people today are either incapable or unwilling to change. In many respects, this is due to lack of motivation – *a motive for action*. People will be more apt to change when they see how it allows them to soar!

> *"You may encounter many defeats, but you must not be defeated. In fact, it may be necessary to encounter the defeats, so you can know who you are."*
>
> - Maya Angelou

Improving Health & Vitality

For some people, the prior chapter may be a bit abstract. What follows will hit closer to home.

~

Substantial dollars and effort are being directed towards improving health and wellness in response to rising healthcare costs. Until now, the focus has been placed on physical behavior change such as proper nutrition, exercise and weight loss – the visible or tangible side. Yet health-related costs have continued to rise at better than three times the rate of inflation.

The American Institute of Stress states that in excess of 70% of medical problems are stress related and preventable.

Stress is a precursor to chronic conditions, such as hypertension, obesity and depression, and accounts for 60-90% of doctor visits. To a degree, this is a symptom of a larger societal problem.

Thanks in part to technological advances, life today has become more stressful in terms of choices, time, pace and demands. Therefore, our ability to live a healthy and vibrant life is a direct result of our ability to inwardly deal with and manage stress.

Health professionals understand that a healthy lifestyle can help people respond to increased levels of stress. What are frequently overlooked are three additional factors of total wellbeing that are needed for optimal balance that resides internally: the emotional, social and spiritual.

> *"The real epidemic in our culture is not just physical heart disease; it's what I call emotional and spiritual heart disease: the sense of loneliness, isolation, and alienation that is so prevalent in our culture because of the breakdown of the social networks that used to give us a sense of connection and community."*
>
> Dr. Dean Ornish,
> in the *Foreword* to the book *Kitchen Table Wisdom*

Emotional Health
Self Growth

To survive in today's interconnected and turbulent world, people have to be able to embrace diverse or opposing perspectives, reconcile differences, and find common ground. Unfortunately, many people find it easier to surround themselves with people who share similar beliefs or views. These like-minded relationships tend to validate people and, to a degree, make them feel in control of their lives. Problems typically arise when belief-systems clash and people lack sufficient self-awareness and/or the ability and willingness to manage their response based on situational differences.

It is not easy. Dealing with conflict or challenging personalities is tough, but it is also necessary. Answers to today's personal and societal problems will be the result of crossbreeding and not inbreeding. And, if willing, people will inwardly grow and evolve by being pushed and challenged, not by running in place.

Situations are constantly changing, therefore relationships must continually evolve. In his national bestseller *Emotional Intelligence*, Daniel Goleman introduced stages of emotional maturity that either facilitate or undermine healthy relationships. Two stages

– self-awareness and self-management – will be introduced here. The next chapter will address Goleman's third stage: social intelligence.

In order to build healthy relationships and effectively deal with opposition, people require **self awareness.** They must learn to look inward for answers. In many cases, the particular situation or person will not change. In this case, the key variable becomes how to react in a purposeful/intentional way that leads to a more productive long-term outcome. Difficult situations or challenging relationships, while frustrating, can act as a mirror into one's inner-self, providing a perpetual source of emotional or self growth. Denying one's innate need for *self* awareness often results in repeatable forms of personal dysfunction, which can significantly influence a person's emotional health.

> *The keenest sorrow is to recognize ourselves as the sole cause of all our adversities.*
> - Sophocles
> Greek tragic dramatist (496 – 406 BC)

When people increase their self-awareness, they find themselves in a better emotional position to **manage** their response. They will be better equipped and willing to revisit historic biases and assumptions; respecting alternative perspectives, beliefs and personalities.

Social Health
Relationships

People are increasingly challenged with the social pressures and interpersonal dynamics found in life. They struggle with the effects of toxic relationships, peer politics, and dealing with social and emotional problems on a daily basis. They find it difficult managing anger, betrayal and confrontation in an effective manner. It gets ugly fast.

Having competence in social and emotional skills is currently reported by professional entities, such as the National Academy of Sciences, to be a predictor of success and happiness throughout life. Social health or intelligence refers to the way that people learn to relate to themselves and connect with others. Sometimes referred to simplistically as "people skills," social intelligence – the ability to effectively connect with

"Whenever you're in conflict with someone, there is one factor that can make the difference between damaging your relationship and deepening it. That factor is attitude."

- William James, Philosopher

or influence others – also involves a certain amount of self-insight and a consciousness of one's own perceptions and reaction patterns. As people become increasingly more self-aware and develop self-management skills, they will be better equipped to effectively deal in a variety of social situations. They will also be in touch with themselves and correspondingly more in tune with the needs of others. They will be in a better position to reconcile differences and find common ground. This will increase their ability to strengthen current relationships and build new ones.

> *To win the respect of intelligent people and the affection of children;*
>
> *To earn the appreciation of honest critics and endure the betrayal of false friends;*
>
> *To find the best in others;*
>
> *To leave the world a bit better;*
>
> *To know even one life has breathed easier because you lived.*
>
> *This is to have succeeded.*
>
> — Ralph Waldo Emerson

Spiritual Health
Sense of Purpose / Contribution

People in developed societies, with their economic or material needs largely met, seek an increased sense of purpose or self-actualization with the knowledge that they are making a difference in the lives of others. This is the definition of spiritual health: commitment to something larger than our own success. When seen this way, spiritual health is the realization that we are constantly being molded and developed internally. While not necessarily easy, we are being prepared to deal with future opportunities and/or challenges that we are currently ill-equipped to deal with.

Some people may find spiritual fulfillment in religion, but it is only one of many ways. Religion and spirituality are not one in the same. Religion helps provide supportive and like-minded communities; whereas spiritual health is about finding meaning and purpose in our life, connecting with the sources that provide strength, hope

> *Pursue a meaningful life, enriched by a sense of connection with and service toward others.*
>
> - Dalai Lama,
> *Beyond Religion*

and inner peace. It is about learning to tune into our inner voice in order to identify what it is that makes you feel whole, alive and connected to the Universe. When do you feel most fulfilled and complete? What gives you inner peace, comfort, strength and harmony?

After years of neglect, one becomes disconnected from their spiritual self and gets lost. Our world is sadly full of lost people, and the consequences of this are seen all around us in the level of addictions, violence, crime, depression, suicide, and lack of compassion and respect for one another. It is never too late to rekindle this facet of our being. The spiritual self has an amazing ability to recover and flourish.

> *"We are not human beings having a spiritual experience. We are spiritual beings having a human experience."*
>
> – Teilhard de Chardin

Live, Work, Play

Up to this point, this book has focused on what we can do to achieve balance. How we can personally find meaning in today's teeter-totter world by investing in our emotional, social and spiritual health. Like many self-help books, it puts the burden of responsibility on each of us as individuals.

While this is not wrong, it is incomplete.

Individually, we are responsible for our attitude, the quality of our relationships, and our commitment to personal growth. We are responsible for how well we work and play with others. We are responsible for finding our inner-compass, our sense of purpose. Going-forward, however, it is now important to switch gears.

Many of our individual choices are influenced by the environment(s) we find ourselves in. In large part, we are by-products of our environment, conditioned by where we live, work and play.

> *"The thing I have learned at IBM is that culture is everything."*
>
> - Louis V. Gerstner, Jr.
> Former CEO IBM

Realizing this, by starting early, as schools expand beyond subject-matter proficiency, our children can become more self-aware and resilient, inwardly prepared to find purpose and constructively interact with others. For many other people, work is another fertile source of personal development. Learning how to constructively deal with challenging personalities, opposing viewpoints and stressful circumstances will provide infinite opportunities for inner-growth.

The point is the quality, consistency and values of our environment – school or work – has a profound impact on our individual ability to achieve balance and find meaning. Businesses, nonprofits and schools are workplaces; the quality of which is determined by the effectiveness and cohesiveness of their leaders.

> *"If you have been trying to make changes in how your organization works, you need to find out how the existing culture aids or hinders you ... The only thing of real importance that leaders do is to create and manage culture."*
>
> - Edgar Schein, professor
> MIT Sloan School of Management

Why Work, Why Now

Today's workplaces offer fertile ground for personal and societal improvement. The fact is, many people are physically and mentally depleted when they leave work. The effects of stress and challenging work relationships leave people emotionally and socially drained, and people who lack a strong sense of purpose fail to tap into infinite reservoirs of spiritual energy. As a result many people are frustrated, exhausted, unhappy and unfilled. This is neither healthy nor sustainable. Organizations are living communities. They require a vibrant, resilient and productive workforce. They require people skilled at reconciling differences, dealing with variation and finding creative solutions buried amongst diverse viewpoints.

> *Nearly 50% of American workers are dissatisfied at work, actively disengaged from their jobs.*
> According to separate surveys conducted by Gallup and Conference Board

Positive energy generated at work will influence society, and thereby make families and communities stronger. It is logical: the more that people are valued and experience the positive effects of encouragement, teamwork, support and even love, the more apt they are to extend positive energy to others. As people achieve a greater degree of balance, they will learn to respect diversity, reconcile differences, and get along with people unlike themselves. As a result, the world in and outside of work will dramatically improve.

~

This book is not offering a new idea; it is suggesting a balanced approach that is rooted in the wisdom of humankind's most renowned philosophers. Many well-intentioned initiatives, attempting to humanize the workplace by putting people before profits, have struggled for acceptance. This has led some organizations to shift completely to the other side of the pendulum in the belief that looking at profits alone is the answer. A more balanced method would achieve both goals in a sustainable manner that simultaneously improves financial health and workforce effectiveness and vitality. In part, this book highlights the impact on individuals; but more importantly, it will introduce what leaders must do to create a meaningful and productive work environment. In this way, we can cultivate organizations that tap into infinite, albeit latent, sources of emotional, social and spiritual energy.

> *If it was easy, everyone would be doing it.*

"Without a doubt, financial factors like pay and benefits are a vital part of the employment deal, but employers need to consider and manage the full range of factors to ensure that their workforce is engaged."

According to *Mercer's* October 2011 *What's Working* survey

"Engagement is not satisfaction or happiness, but the degree to which workers connect to the company emotionally, and are aware of what they need to do to add value."

According to a worldwide survey conducted by Towers Perrin

A new world is rapidly forming, driven in large part by today's global and interconnected marketplace, therefore success, actually survival, awaits those people and organizations capable of adapting to it.

- Thomas L. Friedman, Author
The World Is Flat: A Brief History of the Twenty-First Century

Bringing Meaning into Monday™
A Sustainable Approach to Bottom Line Success

In the 1500s, Martin Luther boldly proposed that work was a way of serving a higher purpose beyond self – an act similar to worship. John Calvin further advanced this line of thinking. In fact, he has been credited with planting the first seeds of capitalism. For Calvin, work was like ministry. He believed that people had a right to do meaningful work; work that allowed them to make a positive difference in the lives of others.

Now, five hundred years later, in 2009, Harvard established "The MBA Oath" – a Hippocratic Oath for business, which reads, "my purpose is to serve the greater good by bringing people and resources together to create value that no single individual can create alone."

~

Meaningful, purpose-driven work is satisfying because it is rooted in basic human needs: using our talents, individually and collectively, *to produce something of value for others*. In part, this value is a result of *what* we provide (e.g., products, programs, services). It is also a direct result of *how* well we provide it (e.g., teamwork, integrity, creativity, responsiveness).

Emphasizing value creation and delivery will simultaneously affect performance and employee well-being, elements that every organization is looking for ways to improve.

Certainly, individuals are a significant part of the answer. Yet, for this to occur, today's leaders must create a cohesive, unifying and clear sense of purpose aimed at continually improving the product and/or service value that their team, department or organization delivers to others.

"Companies must enable their employees to pitch and run with new ideas ... make meaning for their employees and allow them the chance to align their personal values with what they do on the job everyday."

- Stuart L. Hart, Author
Capitalism at the Crossroads

Impact on Me
Impact on personal health, energy and vitality

This book introduced the need for increased balance; showing how it will improve health, energy and vitality. The purpose going-forward is to demonstrate how a value-based work climate can be a big part of the answer.

Individuals, working within a team or work environment that promotes balance, value and unity, will simultaneously experience healthier relationships (social health); greater resiliency (emotional health); increased energy (physical health); and a greater sense of purpose or contribution (spiritual health).

Healthier Relationships

Given today's complexities, in order to produce value, people must develop the social agility and interpersonal tact to play well with others. Reframing an individual's interpersonal approach will have a profound and lasting impact, in and outside of work.

Greater Resiliency

Like it or not, creativity yields conflict. People, therefore, must develop the skills or personal resiliency to better deal with diverse views and the everyday stresses of work. Organizations will create a more fluid and resilient work environment by aligning the workforce around the shared goal of producing value. In this context, individuals will be willing to consider new insights and/or divergent perspectives, and discard historic practices or beliefs that no longer add value.

Increased Energy

In order to improve physical health or energy, people are primarily encouraged to eat right and get active. A unified, value-based workplace will also substantially improve health and energy by tapping into human abilities in a more balanced and holistic manner.

Sense of Purpose or Contribution

By emphasizing value – directing resources and services toward serving the needs and priorities of others – people will have a shared and more focused sense of how to contribute productively, both personally and collectively.

> *"70 percent of our total energy is emotional – the kind that manifests as hope, resilience, passion, fun, and enthusiasm."*
>
> - Mira Kirshenbaum, Author
> *The Emotional Energy Factor*

The Role of Leadership

But the story doesn't end there. Individuals, even if they are one-hundred percent committed to serving others, are only part of the answer. Today's leaders must create work environments that reduce conflicts, remove barriers, and reconcile differences. To be successful, leaders must establish a unifying and clear sense of purpose by streamlining work practices and increasing trust, cooperation, accountability and ownership.

People have unlimited capacity, and the best leaders create an environment that allows them to discover and tap into it. To remain engaged, employees require more than fair pay and opportunities for advancement. Effective leaders, by providing employees a better line-of-sight relative to how they or their teams contribute value, will trigger intrinsic motivators.

> *Creating value is an inherently cooperative process ... people can't act in isolation.*

People will feel more connected and emotionally engaged. This, in turn, will result in more committed, cooperative and responsive workers. Relationships will improve, and conflicting self-interests will be better resolved in the context of a shared purpose that aligns individual agendas with team, department or organizational priorities.

Effective leadership extends beyond visibility, charisma and interpersonal traits. Quite often, the best leaders will choose to go unnoticed because, when the work is done, their employees will say they did it themselves. The best leaders achieve more with less by creating an empowered and collaborative work environment that results in a greater degree of motivational balance – between performance and people – by emphasizing value and building unity.

> "The real core competence of companies will be the ability to continuously and creatively destroy and remake themselves to meet customer demands ... this requires an organization that isn't built to last but one that is built to change."
>
> - Noel M. Tichy, Author
> *The Leadership Engine*

Achieving More with Less

Suffice to say, most people have good intentions. They go to work with the desire to work hard and get along with others. They want to contribute value and use their time constructively. Yet, many of the same people are unable to keep up. This is not necessarily due to lack of commitment, but instead due to a lack of focus and prioritization. As a result, they are unclear as to what activities add value, and which do not.

Today, many people are attempting to be everything to everybody. They are unable to assess importance and differentiate between high- or low-value requests. Not all requests or demands are of equal value, nor are all requestors of equal importance. Similarly, not all customers or coworkers want the same thing or desire to be treated in the same way. Creating value does not imply doing everything for everybody. Instead, it is a proactive way to plan ahead, aligning strategies, resources and people

> *One in three American workers are chronically overworked and 54% have felt overwhelmed at some point in the last month.*
>
> Families and Work Institute

in the most effective and efficient fashion. People require the ability to make consistent and timely trade-off decisions. Leaders have to enable this to occur. Having good people does not guarantee a strong organization; ensuring good people are focused on the right things does.

> *"The significant problems we face cannot be solved by the same level of thinking that created them."*
>
> – Albert Einstein

The Essence of Work – Creating Value

Successful individuals, teams and organizations make it a priority to understand the needs and priorities of their customers, internal clients, patients or students. As such, their primary objective is to determine what their clientele value and what they do not. In this way, their goal is to improve the effectiveness in how they serve them.

> *"Work should give substance, meaning, and value to our lives ... help us focus not on ourselves but others."*
>
> - Michael Hammer, Author
> *Beyond Re-Engineering*

Excitement and motivation for work increases the more people have a clear understanding of how their efforts provide value to others. They will identify creative ways to optimize and generate additional value if they know where to focus. In order to achieve the above, leaders must:

- **Provide direction or clarity:** Converting plans into execution – establishing goals and accountability.
- **Define core values / image**: Ensuring consistency within and outside the organization.

➤ **Manage service levels:** Not all customers, clients, patients or students require the same things nor do they prefer to be treated the same way.

➤ **Optimize work practices:** Proactively assess key work processes in order to improve value, teamwork and consistency.

As leaders systematically address the above elements, they will better align the efforts of their workers. People will be more engaged, cooperative and productive. They will be better equipped to achieve more with less, delivering more value with less effort.

> *""There is nothing wrong with pursuing a vision for greatness ... the good to great companies continually refined the path to greatness with the brutal facts of reality."*
>
> – Jim Collins, Author,
> *Good to Great*

Getting on the Same Page – Unity

In order to produce value, many well-intentioned, albeit diverse or even opposing perspectives and ideas must be considered and resolved. Getting everyone on the same page is a key role of leaders.

To survive today, individuals and organizations have to become less provincial by not protecting historic mindsets or turf. Many authors and thought-leaders have been pointing toward the answer: the need for increased interdependence and collaboration. This is not difficult to grasp. The challenge is doing it. In these transitional times, leadership is about building unity and providing people with hope and direction – a positive sense of the future and what is required to achieve it.

> *"Transformation in thinking from 'I' to 'we' is the most important process leaders go through ... recognizing the unlimited potential of empowered people working together toward a shared purpose."*
>
> - Bill George, Author
> *True North*

People are social creatures, not machines. As such, they are intrinsically seeking a stronger sense of emotional connection or purpose. Therefore, leaders would be wise to consider creating a work environment that fosters this. In addition to improving operational performance, instilling a more service / value-oriented work climate will build unity and a greater degree of connection and contribution.

> *An organization that emphasizes the importance of individual contributions to organizational success will be most successful. ... Leaders must provide structures that support cooperation.*
>
> The National Institute of Occupational Safety and Health, in a 2005 workplace study

Going Forward

Outside of work, people can selectively gravitate toward people who share similar ideals, beliefs and interests. Showing compassion, support, respect, even love, is more natural.

At work, one cannot always choose their friends and/or situation. They are interacting with people who may not share similar beliefs, have historic or cultural biases, and all too often, are pursuing conflicting agendas. At work, egos and self-interests collide; fueled by the need for control, status and material gain. Ironically, at work, these traits are even rewarded and justified within the context of growth and profit.

Social altruism is not the answer. Many well-intentioned, well-designed initiatives have not been sustainable. Why? Because of failure to show a clear and measurable bottom-line connection. In order to develop a more compassionate and meaningful workplace, we must rally the support of today's organizational leaders by appealing to their ego-centric, bottom-line agendas.

Adam Smith, who many people see as the originator of capitalism, in 1776, defined the "invisible hand" of capitalism: *achieving wealth by improving the well-being of society.* By appealing to mankind's self-interests, Smith showed how people could improve their standard of living, yet in a manner that simultaneously improved the well-being of others. Viewed this way, capitalism works. It is not sustainable, however, when capitalism is narrowly defined as simply the ability to make money, regardless of the social outcome. Emphasizing value creation is not a new-age way to succeed; instead it reawakens a more proven and sustainable way – *achieving financial health by improving societal well-being.*

The purpose of this book was to connect-the-dots by showing how improving results in a value-added manner will simultaneously achieve greater balance, build unity and improve employee health, energy and vitality. Individuals, intrinsically, will become more energized & engaged as they deepen their emotional, social and spiritual connection to others and experience a greater sense of purpose, hope and community.

> *"People are looking for leaders of any kind ... who will offer ideas on what needs to be done, and bring others together."*
>
> - Rich Harwood, Author, *Hope Unraveled*

A Picture Says a 1000 Words

The graphic on the facing page helps summarize the contents and objectives of this book. As represented by the bolded scale in the center, this graphic reflects the need for balance. The first few chapters of this book outline the same reality: that greater balance – emotional, social and spiritual – will improve our individual health and vitality.

The graphic reflects the broader impact that living a balanced lifestyle can have on our lives, families, organizations and communities. Similar to this book, this graphic emphasizes the importance of our school and work environments. Due to the amount of time spent at these places, they play a significant role in our ability to achieve balance and find meaning. One's ability to do so is, in part, a direct reflection of the quality of the environment that their leaders foster.

Finally, the left side of this graphic reminds us of our individual commitment to self improvement. To remain relevant, we must continually reinvent ourselves. Outwardly, we do so in terms of cultivating marketable skills. Inwardly or behaviorally, we can reinvent ourselves in terms of improving upon our resiliency and self-awareness. Due to the proliferation and accessibility of self help or support-based resources, this book does not expand on these points in greater detail.

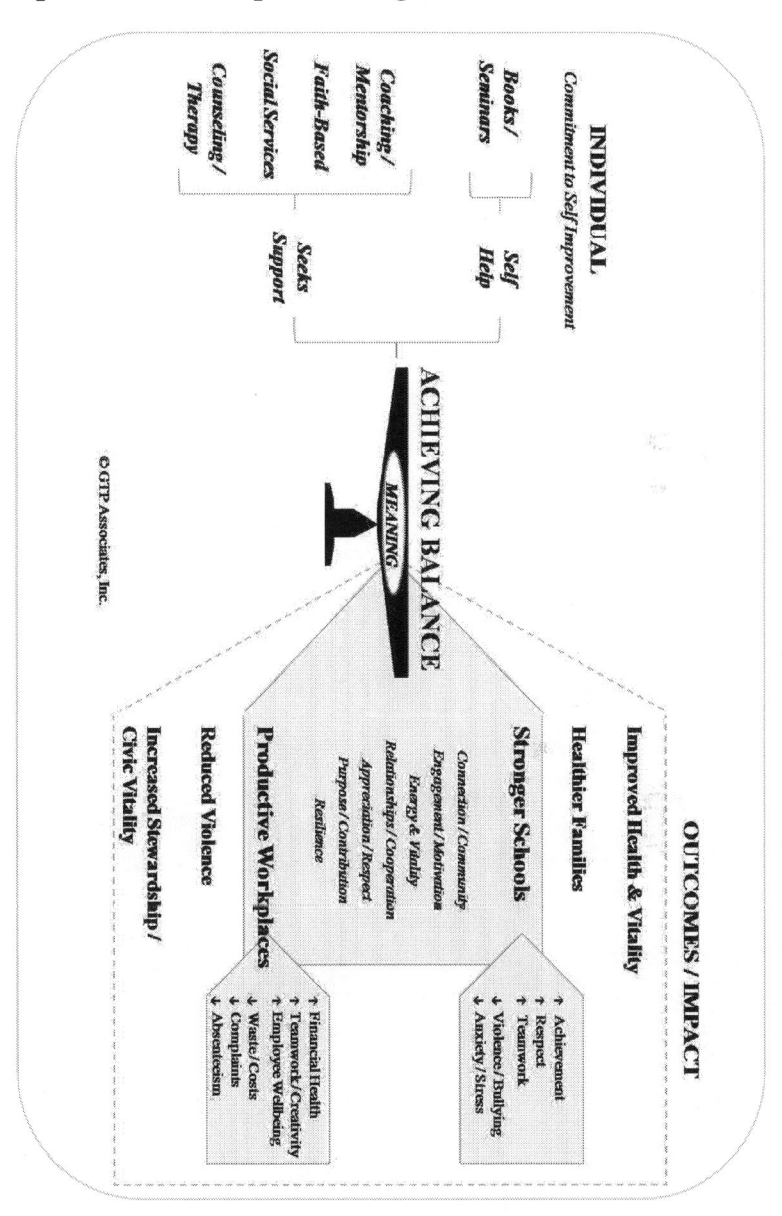

INDIVIDUAL
Commitment to Self Improvement

- Books / Seminars
- Coaching / Mentorship
- Faith-Based
- Social Services
- Counseling / Therapy

Self Help

Seeks Support

ACHIEVING BALANCE

MEANING

- Healthier Families
  - Connection / Community
  - Engagement / Motivation
  - Energy & Vitality
  - Relationships / Cooperation
  - Appreciation / Respect
  - Purpose / Contribution
  - Resilience
- Stronger Schools
  - → Achievement
  - → Respect
  - → Teamwork
  - ← Violence / Bullying
  - ← Anxiety / Stress
- Productive Workplaces
  - → Financial Health
  - → Teamwork / Creativity
  - → Employee Wellbeing
  - ← Waste / Costs
  - ← Complaints
  - ← Absenteeism
- Reduced Violence
- Increased Stewardship / Civic Vitality

OUTCOMES / IMPACT

Improved Health & Vitality

© GTP Associates, Inc.

A Closing Word

Society itself is nothing but a collection of individuals. It follows that if we want to change society, it is up to each one of us to make our contribution. While respecting our external differences, we must promote inner values that are universal – embracing cultural, racial, religious and humanist perspectives so that we can work together as individuals.

Developing ones inner-values and respecting our shared humanity and interdependence takes time. It is reliant on intuition and introspection. People tend to learn via everyday experiences. Therefore, inner-growth should also occur where people spend the majority of their time: where relationships and attitudes are conditioned.

> *"It's the action, not the fruit of the action, that's important. You have to do the right thing ... if you do nothing, there will be no result."*
> — Mahatma Gandhi

In virtually all jobs, people are faced with challenging personalities, diverse beliefs, opposing viewpoints and stressful circumstances. Learning how to constructively deal with this reality provides an infinite opportunity for inner-growth and positively affects individual health, families and communities. In addition to improved performance and energized employees, organizations will experience a greater sense of unity and rediscover a more sustainable route to success. This will improve the well-being of society by providing a template for healthy social/emotional interaction.

> *"It seems we may live in a society that has almost forgotten the glory of what it means to be human. We are in need of healing."*
>
> - M. Scott Peck, M.D., Author,
> *A World Waiting to be Born: Civility Rediscovered*

Note from the Author

This book focused on finding meaning: *why* balance is important to our individual health and vitality, and *how* it can be achieved at work. In this way, this book is a prequel to a book I authored in 2009, *Bringing Meaning into Monday: A Sustainable Approach to Bottom Line Success*, which drills deeper into *what* organizations can do to build a healthy foundation that results in a more productive, vibrant, resilient and meaningful workplace. In particular, *what* leaders can do to foster it by:

Building trust and accountability
Establishing a greater sense of shared purpose
Streamlining work practices and services
Tapping diverse talent

Excerpt from *Bringing Meaning into Monday: A Sustainable Approach to Bottom Line Success:*

> ... paradigms must be shifted, and beliefs, mindsets and work practices must be redefined. The global marketplace will continue to evolve and change, therefore, today's organizations must be able to evolve and grow. This implies that leaders must be skilled at leading change. In addition to developing their own personal resiliency and self-awareness, they must be equipped – intellectually and emotionally – to lead others through the turbulence of a changing world. Their ability to deliver bottom-line results is dependent on it, as is the sanity, effectiveness and sense of hope of those they lead.

A third book for this *meaning* series, tentatively titled *Achieving Meaning at Work: Creating Change from the Bottom Up,* is currently underway, and is scheduled for publication in early 2014.

By applying the same two-page chapter format used in this book, this third book will help leaders implement the concepts introduced in my first two books in an affordable and sustainable manner. As the title suggests, the book will outline how organizations can apply a *bottom up* approach to change that is grounded in proven and practical principles.

In large part, the concepts I've shared in my first two books are rooted in universal principles, applicable within all types and sizes of organizations. With that said, worthwhile efforts take time and discipline. This third book will describe how to effectively manage this transition by initially applying concepts to a small number of existing teams and/or efforts. In this way, concepts become seeded within an organization and broader application will be a natural result of internal champions and stories emerging.

What follows is the introduction from *Achieving Meaning at Work: Creating Change from the Bottom Up.*

Tentative release in 2014 or sooner:

Achieving Meaning at Work

Creating Change from the Bottom Up

When people first hear about the possibility of increased balance and/or achieving a greater inner-sense of meaning and happiness in life, they are rather skeptical. To a large extent, our beliefs and attitudes have been conditioned by being emersed in a "more is better" society and by an endless parade of self-help gurus. We tend to believe that happiness and meaning is a result of where we live or what we do, drive, own and wear. In part, it is. However, if we do not also acknowledge our intrinsic or spiritual nature as human beings, we ultimately miss the mark.

My experience has been that this skepticism is easily overcome. This is because most people have an innate understanding that there is more to life than earning potential.

What I've found to be more difficult is getting people to accept that improving today's workplaces are a big part of the answer. In my experience, their reluctance or cynicism is not because they don't agree that a holistic model of management would inherently be more productive. Instead, is is due to one or more of the following factors:

- **People** resist change. In particular, they avoid deep changes that affect their inner-self.
- **Organizations** are focused heavily on results and tend to be neglectful of the human element.
- **Current leaders** often lack in communication and empathy skills, and in their ability to inspire and empower others. This can compromise their ability to command trust and respect.

Given the above perceptions, who can blame people for avoiding change? Frankly, they're often right: many efforts to improve work environments miss the mark. Taken seperately, each factor above will derail most well-intentioned improvement efforts. In truth, these factors are interconnected. Failing to acknowledge them will compromise the best intentions.

Over 70% of change initiatives fail.

According to separate research conducted by Kotter, McKinsey, and Blanchard

This book will improve the odds of success. It prompts people to make practical improvements as individuals, as leaders, and as teams. As concepts are put into practice, they will naturally spread further. People are smart; they know a good thing when they see it.

About the Author

Mark D. Sauter is the founder and president of GTP Associates, Inc., a Michigan-based firm specializing in organizational improvement in terms of performance, leadership effectiveness and employee well-being. With over 25 years of business leadership experience, Mark's work, while with Dow Corning Corporation, was profiled in *Value Based Marketing for Bottom-Line Success* – McGraw-Hill, 2003. In 2009, Mark released his first book entitled *Bringing Meaning Into Monday™: A Sustainable Approach to Bottom Line Success* – available on Amazon.com.

About GTP Associates

Growth **T**hrough **P**eople – develops human potential in a reinforcing and sustainable manner. In addition to **client-specific** support, GTP Associates has established a **community-based** delivery model that can cost effectively assist multiple organizations/teams, simultaneously. Information is available at www.gtpassociates.com.

ORDER ADDITIONAL COPIES

Finding Meaning in a Teeter-Totter World

1-49 copies	$7.95 each @ Amazon.com	
50-499 copies	$7.50 each	contact us @
500-999 copies	$7.00 each	www.gtpassociates.com
1000 or more copies	$6.50 each	

Bringing Meaning into Monday: A Sustainable Approach to Bottom Line Success [132p]

1-49 copies	$14.95 each @ Amazon.com	
50-499 copies	$13.75 each	contact us @
500-999 copies	$12.50 each	www.gtpassociates.com
1000 or more copies	$11.25 each	

Achieving Meaning at Work: Creating Change from the Bottom Up   [available in 2014]

Applicable sales tax, shipping and handling charges will be added. Prices subject to change.

GTP ASSOCIATES can introduce *MEANING* within your organization or community in the following ways: Keynotes; Webinars; Workshops; Applied via 100-day team-based process.

> *We believe* that many organizations, teams and individuals have a significant amount of untapped potential. *Our approach* is to show leaders how this potential can be identified, unified and focused. *Our results* are measurable, repeatable, and time-driven in terms of improved performance, inspired workforce, and more vibrant communities.
>
> Additional information is available at www.gtpassociates.com.

Made in the USA
Charleston, SC
29 March 2013